ALTERNATOR
BOOKS™

SPACE IN ACTION

BLACK HOLES IN ACTION

An AUGMENTED REALITY Experience

Kevin Kurtz

T0386293

Lerner Publications ◆ Minneapolis

explore space in brand-new ways with augmented reality!

1. Ask a parent or guardian for permission to download the free Lerner AR app on your digital device by going to the App Store or Google Play.

2. As you read, look for this icon throughout the book. It means there is an augmented reality experience on that page!

3. Use the Lerner AR app to scan the picture near the icon.

4. Watch space come alive with augmented reality!

CONTENTS

INTRODUCTION
STAR DESTROYER

The black hole at the center of the Milky Way **galaxy**, Sagittarius A*, is destroying stars. It pulls them in with its enormous **gravity**. Stars circle the black hole until they disappear forever.

Sagittarius A* is about four million times the **mass** of the sun. Everything in our galaxy **orbits** it, including millions of other black holes. They pull in nearby objects, and some black holes crash into other black holes.

This illustration shows the Milky Way from afar (*left*) and the region near Sagittarius A*.

Scientists captured the first image of a black hole's event horizon at the center of the Messier 87 galaxy.

Black holes exist all around the universe. They have incredible amounts of matter packed inside a small space. Their enormous mass gives black holes more gravity than anything else in the universe has. Even light cannot escape their pull. Since we need light to see, black holes are invisible. So how do we know about them?

Modern technology allows us to see evidence of black holes. In 2019 NASA released the first picture of a black hole's **event horizon**. The image shows a black hole in action doing some of the most incredible things in the universe.

BLACK HOLES eat STARS

G as swirls like a whirlpool as a black hole rips apart a star. The spinning gas's temperature rises to millions of degrees. Some of the gas disappears into the black hole. The rest spins so fast that it shoots into space.

Sagittarius A* is surrounded by massive clouds of hot gas.

Jets of light and energy stream into
space as a black hole destroys a star.

A star is a giant ball of hot gas. If a star gets too close to a
black hole, the black hole's gravity pulls on the near side of
a star with more force than the far side. This pulls the star
apart. It flows into the black hole as a stream of gas.

The plummeting gas reaches speeds close to one-third the
speed of light. This heats up the gas and causes it to release
tremendous amounts of light and energy. The light lets us
see what black holes are doing.

A RANGE OF ENERGY

Energy travels through space at the speed of light in waves. A wavelength is the distance between the top of one wave and the top of the next wave. The **electromagnetic spectrum** is a range of energy types with different wavelengths. The spectrum includes **X-rays**, gamma waves, infrared waves, and others.

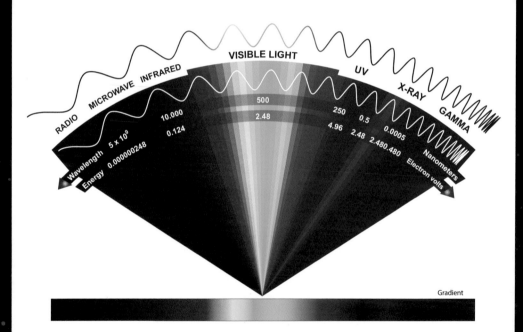

Most of the electromagnetic spectrum is invisible to humans.

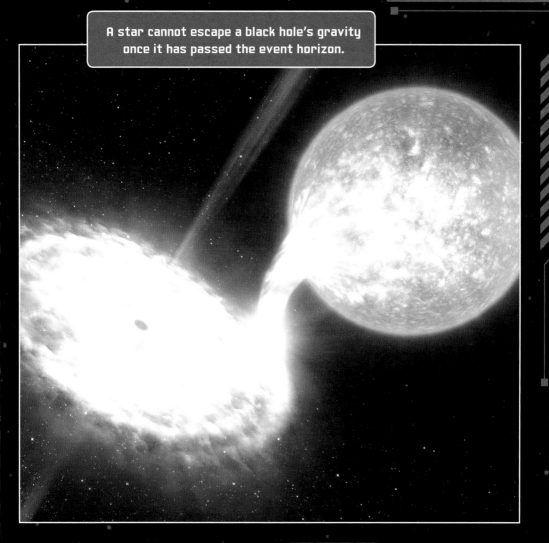

   Some of these waves of light have wavelengths that allow us to see them. Others are invisible to humans without special telescopes. These high-tech devices provide information about distant events in the universe, such as what happens when black holes eat stars.

a BLACK HOLE IS BORN

On June 16, 2018, telescopes around the world saw an object in space one hundred billion times brighter than the sun. They named it AT2018cow, or the Cow. At first, **astronomers** weren't sure what such a bright object could be.

When black holes eat stars, they give off massive X-ray energy that astronomers on Earth can observe with special telescopes.

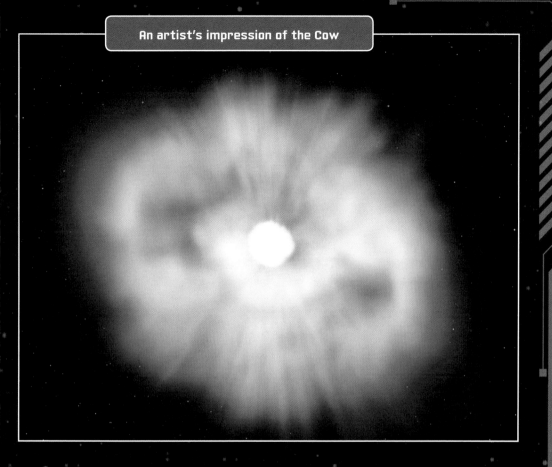

An artist's impression of the Cow

After analyzing data from the Cow, astronomers think it may have been a black hole destroying a very dense star such as a white dwarf. A white dwarf has a lot of matter squeezed into a small space. When a black hole rips apart a white dwarf, the black hole ejects an enormous amount of material. The jet of material from a white dwarf could appear as bright as the Cow did on June 16.

Another theory is that the light came from a **supernova**. Supernovas are among the brightest objects in the universe. When these huge star explosions occur, they can form new black holes.

Astronomers discovered supernova SN 1998bw (*bright dot at the arrow*) in 1998.

THE EXPLOSIVE BIRTH OF BLACK HOLES

Supernovas are explosions of huge stars that are much more massive than the sun. These gigantic stars blow up when they run out of fuel. With no fuel, the center of the star collapses and explodes. The explosion creates light that astronomers can observe.

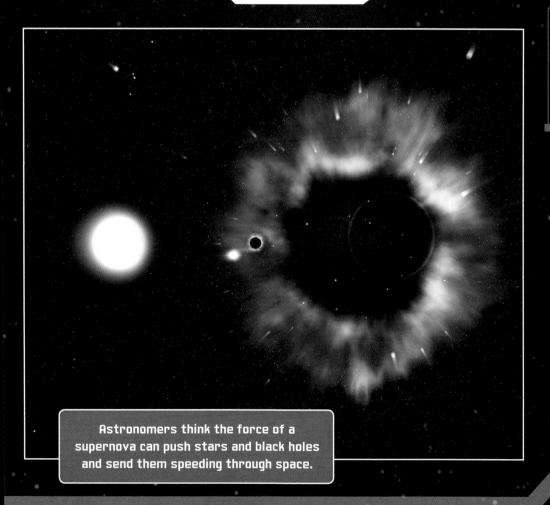

Astronomers think the force of a supernova can push stars and black holes and send them speeding through space.

A supernova gives off X-rays, gamma rays, and other forms of energy.

The gravity of the collapsed star becomes more intense as it pulls in more matter. Eventually, even light cannot escape from it. A black hole is born.

THE LESS EXPLOSIVE BIRTH OF BLACK HOLES

Not all black holes are born with a bang. Some form when stars fizzle out. In 2015 telescopes observed a huge star that seemed to disappear suddenly. No one was sure what had happened.

The image on the left of star N6946-BH1 is from 2007. When astronomers looked at the same location in 2015, the star had vanished.

The Hubble Space Telescope has orbited Earth since 1990.

In 2017 astronomers used the Hubble Space Telescope to get a closer look. Hubble can observe visible, ultraviolet, and infrared light from its place in orbit about 340 miles (547 km) above Earth. The telescope would be able to pick up extremely faint light in any of those wavelengths coming from the star that had disappeared.

Instead of a dim star, Hubble saw empty space. But that didn't mean nothing was there. Astronomers think the huge star collapsed into a black hole without the fireworks of a supernova. This way of creating black holes may be common. As many as 30 percent of massive stars might just fizzle out to form black holes. Scientists aren't sure why some stars become supernovas and others don't.

Supernova SN 1987A exploded with the power of one hundred million suns.

CHAPTER 3

WATCHING BLACK HOLES

Soaring 86,500 miles (139,208 km) above Earth's surface, the Chandra X-ray Observatory watches black holes by collecting X-rays. The cutting-edge telescope is in orbit because Earth's atmosphere absorbs X-rays from space. An X-ray telescope would not work on Earth's surface.

Earth's atmosphere is hundreds of miles thick.

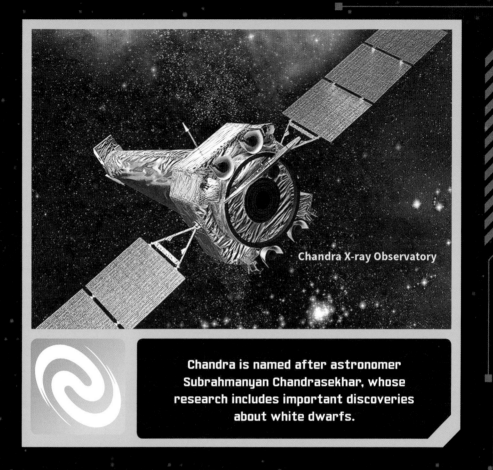

Chandra X-ray Observatory

Chandra is named after astronomer Subrahmanyan Chandrasekhar, whose research includes important discoveries about white dwarfs.

Chandra has a system of mirrors that direct X-rays to special instruments that record data. Computers use the X-ray data to create color images. They show things we can't see with other telescopes. Chandra contributed X-ray data to the first image of the black hole event horizon that NASA released in 2019.

Chandra has also captured data from a supermassive black hole more than 730 million **light-years** away. It is in the center of the Cygnus A galaxy. Chandra observed what happens when a supermassive black hole eats a star.

Jets of energy created by a supermassive black hole appear above and below the Centaurus A galaxy.

When a black hole captures a star, most of the star is pulled into the black hole. But some of the spinning matter speeds up so quickly that it shoots away into space, creating jets of particles and energy that release X-rays. X-rays from jets near Cygnus A reached Chandra in 2016. The data allowed astronomers to learn more about how black holes work.

BLACK HOLES RULE GALAXIES

Scientists think all galaxies have a supermassive black hole at their center. These black holes are millions to billions of times more massive than the sun. They have so much gravity that the rest of the galaxy revolves around them. In 2018 astronomers proved the Milky Way's center is a supermassive black hole, Sagittarius A*. Chandra found evidence that as many as twenty thousand black holes may orbit within 3 light-years of the Milky Way's center.

Billions of star systems made up of planets, comets, and other objects orbit Sagittarius A*, the supermassive black hole at the center of the Milky Way.

an astronomy REVOLUTION

T wo black holes are caught in each other's gravity. They move closer and closer before colliding in a violent crash. Then they merge to form an even larger black hole. Black hole collisions are some of the most powerful events in the universe. But until recently, astronomers had no way to observe them.

This image of two supermassive black holes merging was created by a computer. Scientists use computer simulations to learn more about objects such as black holes that we can't observe directly.

Moving objects produce **gravitational waves**. Even you produce gravitational waves when you move around, though yours are too small to feel. These waves are not part of the electromagnetic spectrum. They are like ripples that travel through space. Gravitational waves from violent events such as black hole collisions can travel trillions of miles to reach Earth. They pass through our planet every day, but by the time they reach us, they are so small that we don't even notice them.

Two black holes orbit each other before colliding. Scientists created this image to show what black holes might look like to humans if we could get close enough to observe their effects directly.

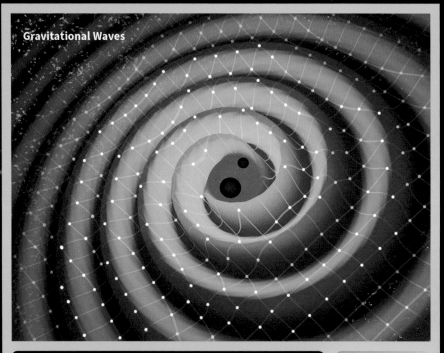

Gravitational Waves

As black holes orbit each other, they create a spiral pattern of gravitational waves in space.

In 1916 Albert Einstein predicted that gravitational waves exist, but no one proved it until recently. Scientists from around the world built the Laser Interferometer Gravitational-Wave Observatory in 1999 to detect gravitational waves. The waves can be thousands of times smaller than a **proton** by the time they reach Earth. The observatory is like a huge antenna that can pick up these tiny waves.

In 2015 the observatory detected gravitational waves for the first time. They were from the collision of two black holes. One black hole was thirty-six times the mass of the sun. The other was twenty-nine times the mass of the sun. It was the beginning of a brand-new way to observe the universe.

The Laser Interferometer Gravitational-Wave Observatory facility in Livingston, Louisiana

LISTENING TO THE UNIVERSE

Gravitational waves act like sound waves. Astronomers can turn gravitational waves into sound and hear distant events, such as black hole collisions and supernovas. Before detecting gravitational waves, astronomy was like watching a movie with the sound off. Gravitational wave astronomy is turning the sound on for the universe.

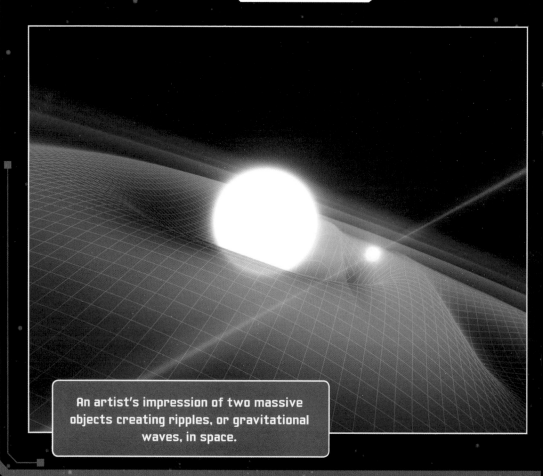

An artist's impression of two massive objects creating ripples, or gravitational waves, in space.

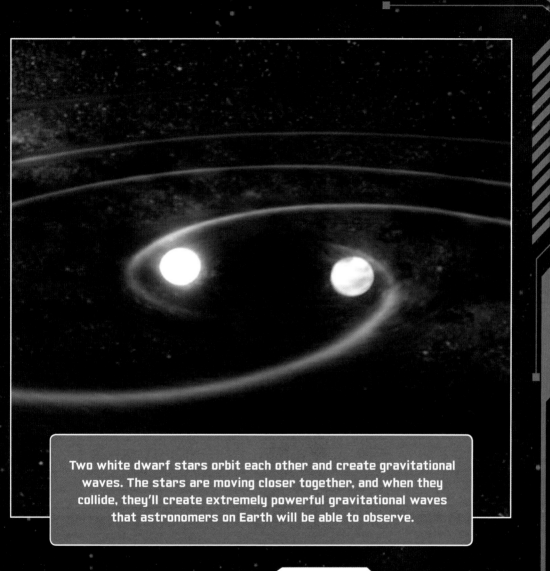

Two white dwarf stars orbit each other and create gravitational waves. The stars are moving closer together, and when they collide, they'll create extremely powerful gravitational waves that astronomers on Earth will be able to observe.

Gravitational wave detection is a new form of astronomy. It will teach us many things, not only about black holes but also about other aspects of our amazing universe. We may even discover new objects in the universe that we can't see, but we can hear.

Follow the links below to download 3D printer files for some of the telescopes in this book.

Chandra X-ray Observatory, http://qrs.lernerbooks.com/Chandra

Hubble Space Telescope, http://qrs.lernerbooks.com/Hubble

James Webb Space Telescope, http://qrs.lernerbooks.com /JamesWebb

astronomers: scientists who study objects and matter in space

electromagnetic spectrum: a range of energy types with different wavelengths

event horizon: the boundary at a black hole beyond which nothing can escape

galaxy: a vast group of stars, planets, and other objects in space. Earth is in the Milky Way galaxy.

gravitational waves: waves set off by the movement of objects in space that spread out like ripples through the universe

gravity: an invisible force that attracts objects to one another

light-years: units of measurement equal to the distance light can travel in one year

mass: the amount of matter in an object

orbits: moves in a path around a body in space

proton: a tiny particle that is part of an atom

supernova: an explosion of a supermassive star

X-rays: waves of energy that are part of the electromagnetic spectrum and that can be detected by special telescopes

Astronomy for Kids: Black Holes
https://www.ducksters.com/science/black_hole.php

Black Hole Fun Facts for Kids
https://www.ouruniverseforkids.com/black-holes/

Dickinson, Terence. *The Hubble Space Telescope: Our Eye on the Universe*. Buffalo: Firefly, 2019.

Kenney, Karen Latchana. *Sound and Light Waves Investigations*. Minneapolis: Lerner Publications, 2018.

Kurtz, Kevin. *Cutting-Edge Black Holes Research*. Minneapolis: Lerner Publications, 2020.

NASA Space Place
https://spaceplace.nasa.gov

National Geographic Kids: Black Holes
https://kids.nationalgeographic.com/explore/space/black
-holes/#black-hole-1.jpg

Roland, James. *Black Holes: A Space Discovery Guide*. Minneapolis: Lerner Publications, 2017.

INDEX

Photo Acknowledgments

Image credits: Freer/Shutterstock.com, p. 2 (bottom); ESA/C. Carreau, p. 4; Event
Horizon Telescope Collaboration, p. 5; NASA/CXC/MIT/F. Baganoff, R. Shcherbakov
et al., p. 6; NASA/CXC/M.Weiss, p. 7; Fouad A. Saad/Shutterstock.com, p. 8; ESA
/Hubble, ESO, M. Kornmesser, p. 9; NASA/JPL-Caltech, pp. 10, 28; NASA/Goddard
Space Flight Center, p. 11; ESO, pp. 12, 14; European Space Agency, NASA and Felix
Mirabel (the French Atomic Energy Commission & the Institute for Astronomy and
Space Physics/Conicet of Argentina), p. 13; NASA, ESA, and C. Kochanek (OSU),
p. 15; NASA, p. 16; NASA/CXC/Penn State/K. Frank et al., p. 17; NASA
/JSC, p. 18; NASA/CXC/SAO, p. 19; ESO/WFI (visible); MPIfR/ESO/APEX/A.Weiss et
al. (microwave); NASA/CXC/CfA/R.Kraft et al. (X-ray), p. 20; MARK GARLICK
/SCIENCE PHOTO LIBRARY/Getty Images, p. 21; NASA/Goddard Space Flight
Center, p. 22; The Simulating eXtreme Spacetimes (SXS) Project/Science Source,
p. 23; T. Pyle/Caltech/MIT/LIGO Lab, p. 24; Caltech/MIT/LIGO Lab, p. 25; ESO/L
. Cal, p. 26; NASA/Goddard Space Flight Center/D. Berry, p. 27. Design elements:
Jetrel/Shutterstock.com; Nanashiro/Shutterstock.com; phiseksit/Shutterstock
.com; MSSA/Shutterstock.com; Pakpoom Makpan/Shutterstock.com; pixelparticle
/Shutterstock.com; wacomka/Shutterstock.com; fluidworkshop/Shutterstock.com.

Cover: Vadim Sadovski/Shutterstock.com.

Lerner Publications Company
An imprint of Lerner Publishing Group, Inc.
241 First Avenue North
Minneapolis, MN 55401 USA

For reading levels and more information, look up this title at www.lernerbooks.com.

Main body text set in Aptifer Sans LT Pro.
Typeface provided by Linotype AG.

Library of Congress Cataloging-in-Publication Data

Names: Kurtz, Kevin, author.
Title: Black holes in action : an augmented reality experience / Kevin Kurtz.
Description: Minneapolis : Lerner Publications, [2020] | Series: Space in action (Alternator books) | Audience: Ages 8–12. | Audience: Grades 4 to 6. | Includes bibliographical references and index.
Identifiers: LCCN 2019010591 (print) | LCCN 2019014072 (ebook) | ISBN 9781541583467 (eb pdf) | ISBN 9781541578807 (lb : alk. paper)
Subjects: LCSH: Black holes (Astronomy)—Juvenile literature. | Gravitational waves—Juvenile literature.
Classification: LCC QB843.B55 (ebook) | LCC QB843.B55 K87 2020 (print) | DDC 523.8/875—dc23

LC record available at https://lccn.loc.gov/2019010591

Manufactured in the United States of America
1-46983-47852-6/25/2019